WINNING
CASINO BLACKJACK
for the
NON-COUNTER

WINNING
CASINO BLACKJACK
for the
NON-COUNTER

Avery D. Cardoza

Cardoza School of Blackjack
P.O. Box 5267
Santa Cruz, California 95063

ISBN:0-9607618-0-2

First Printing   November 1981
Second Printing   February 1982
Third Printing   July 1982

About the Author

Avery Cardoza is the founder of the Cardoza School of Blackjack, a highly successful institute that has trained well over a hundred players in the skills of casino blackjack.

In addition to his teaching skills, Cardoza is known as a world class blackjack player, and has been barred from casinos such as Caesars Palace in Las Vegas. Because of his skills as a player, Cardoza is feared by the major casinos in Nevada and Atlantic City, and must play in disguise or appear incognito when he shows up, ready to play for high stakes.

Cardoza has called upon his years of experience both as a player and teacher to put together this unique book for the non-counting beginner, one that will enable him or her to learn skills necessary to win money at casino blackjack.

To my father

Table of Contents

I. Introduction   4

II. Beginner's Guide to Casino Blackjack   5
Object of the Game • Busting or Breaking • Blackjack • Payoffs •
Card Values • Dealer's Rules • Player's Options • The Play of the
Game • Casino Personnel • Entering a Game • Casino Chips •
Betting • House Limits • Converting Chips into Cash • Free Drinks
and Cigarettes • The Decks of Cards • Rules and Variations of the
Casino Centers (Las Vegas Strip, Downtown Las Vegas, Northern
Nevada, Atlantic City)

III. General Strategic Concepts   13
The Dealer's Only Advantage • Overcoming the Disadvantage of
Acting First • To Beat the Dealer • Understanding the Dealer's Up-
card • Understanding the Player's Hand—Hard Totals

IV. The Optimal Basic Strategies   18
Hitting and Standing • Doubling Down • Splitting Pairs • Single
Deck Master Charts • Nevada Multiple Deck Master Charts •
Atlantic City Multiple Deck Master Charts • Player's Options

V. The Winning Edge   42
Winning Edge • The Cardoza Non-Counter's Strategy • Bet Range
• The Power of our Advantage • Getting the Most out of the Cardoza
Non-Counter Strategy • Tipping • Cheating • Understanding the
Gamble

VI. Money Management   46
Money Management • Bankrolling (Total Bankrolling, Table
Bankroll) • When to Quit (Minimizing Losses, Maximizing Gains)

VII. Glossary   51

List of Tables and Charts

1 Understanding the Dealer's Upcard   16

2 Hitting and Standing—Hard Totals (All Jurisdictions)   18

3 Hitting and Standing—Soft Totals—Northern Nevada (single and multiple deck)   21

4 Hitting and Standing—Soft Totals—Las Vegas and Atlantic City (single and multiple deck)   21

5 Doubling Down—Northern Nevada—Single Deck   24

6 Doubling Down—Las Vegas—Single Deck   24

7 Doubling Down—Northern Nevada—Multiple Deck   25

8 Doubling Down—Atlantic City and Las Vegas— Multiple Deck   25

9 Splitting Pairs—Northern Nevada and Las Vegas— Single Deck   29

10 Splitting Pairs—Northern Nevada and Las Vegas Multiple Deck   29

11 Splitting Pairs—Atlantic City—Multiple Deck   30

12 Master Chart—Northern Nevada Single Deck   34

13 Master Chart—Las Vegas Single Deck   35

14 Master Chart—Northern Nevada Multiple Deck   37

15 Master Chart—Las Vegas Multiple Deck   38

16 Master Chart—Atlantic City Multiple Deck   40

17 Player's Options   41

18 Bankroll Requirements   48

I. Introduction

Blackjack can be beaten! Once you've finished reading this book and learned the skills presented, you'll find that there will be one major difference between you and 95% of the other players—you'll be a winner at blackjack.

We'll teach you to win without the blind memorization and boring tedium usually associated with learning blackjack. Our computer tested basic strategies are carefully explained so that every play you make is easily learned. In addition, all the winning strategies are presented in easy to read charts.

You'll learn how to beat the single deck game without counting cards. Also shown will be the best way to adjust your play for the multiple deck games and variations offered at the Las Vegas, Northern Nevada and Atlantic City casinos.

You'll receive a wealth of information from this book. We cover the fundamentals of casino blackjack—the rules of the game, the players' options, the variations offered in Las Vegas, Northern Nevada and Atlantic City, how to bet, casino vocabulary, how to play and everything else you'll need to know about playing winning casino blackjack.

Not only will we teach you the skills of winning, but just as importantly, we'll teach you how to walk away a winner. Money management is carefully explained to insure your success as a blackjack player. We also discuss emotional control, how to minimize losses when losing, and how to let your winnings ride, so that when you lose, you lose small, and when you win, you win big—the overall result being that you walk away a winner.

For the first time, many of the winning concepts that have been successful taught at the Cardoza School of Blackjack are now presented in book form so that you can win without counting cards.

So read this book carefully, and you'll be among those players that the casinos fear, and for good reason—you will be a consistent winner at blackjack!

II. BEGINNER'S GUIDE TO CASINO BLACKJACK

Object of the Game

The player's object in casino blackjack is to beat the dealer. This can be achieved in two ways:

1—When the player has a higher total than the dealer without exceeding 21.

2—When the dealer's total exceeds 21 (assuming the player has not exceeded 21 first).

In casino blackjack, if the player and the dealer both hold the same total of 21 or less, the hand is a **push**, nobody wins.

Busting or Breaking—Automatic Losers

If the drawing of additional cards to the initial two cards dealt causes the point total to exceed 21, then that hand is said to be **busted**, an automatic loss. Busted hands should be turned up immediately. Once the player has busted, his hand is lost, even if the dealer busts as well afterwards. If the dealer busts, all remaining players automatically win their bets.

Blackjack—Automatic Winner

If the original two card hand contains an Ace with any 10 or face card (J,Q,K), the hand is called a **blackjack**, or **natural**, and is an automatic winner for the player whose bet is paid off at 3 to 2. If the dealer gets a blackjack, all players lose their bets. (The dealer wins only the player's bet, not the 3 to 2 payoff the player receives for a blackjack). If both the dealer and the player are dealt a blackjack, the hand is a push. Blackjacks should be turned up immediately.

Payoffs

All bets are paid off at even money ($5 bet wins $5), except in cases where the player receives a blackjack which is a 3 to 2 payoff ($5 bet wins $7.50) or when the player exercises an option that allows him to double his bet. In these instances (doubling, splitting), the payoff is equal to the new doubled bet. If a bet is doubled from $5 to $10, a win would pay off $10.

Card Values

Each card is counted at face value. 2 = 2 points, 3 = 3 points . . . 10 = 10 points. The face cards, Jack, Queen and King, are counted as 10 points. The Ace can be counted as 1 point or 11 points at the player's discretion. When the Ace is counted as 11 points, that hand is called soft, as in the hand Ace, 7 = soft 18. All other totals, including hands where the Ace counts as 1 point, are called hard (10, 6, A = hard 17).

The dealer must count his Ace as 11 if that gives him a hand totalling 17 to 21, otherwise he must count the Ace as 1 point. In some casinos the rules dictate that the dealer must draw on soft 17. In these casinos the dealer's Ace will count as 1 point when combined with cards totalling 6 points, and the dealer will have to draw until he forms a hand of at least hard 17.

Dealer's Rules

The dealer must play by prescribed guidelines. He must draw to any hand 16 or below and stand on any total 17-21. As mentioned above, some casinos require the dealer to draw on soft 17. The dealer has no options and cannot deviate from the above-stated rules.

Player's Options

Unlike the dealer, the player can vary his strategy. After receiving his first two cards the player has the following options:

1—Drawing (Hitting)

If the player is not satisfied with his two card total he can draw additional cards. To draw a card, the player scrapes the felt surface with his cards, scraping toward his body. In a game where both the player's cards are dealt face up, he scratches the felt with his index finger or points toward the cards if he desires a hit. A player is not supposed to handle the cards when they're face up.

2—Standing

When a player is satisfied with his original two card total, and does not wish to draw additional cards, he signals this by sliding his cards face down under his bet. When the cards are dealt face up, the player indicates his decision to stand pat by waving his hand palm down over his cards.

3—Doubling Down

This option allows the player to double his original bet, in which case he must draw one additional card to his hand and cannot draw any additional cards thereafter. To double down, the player turns his cards face up, and places them in front of his bet. Then he takes an amount equal to his original bet and places those chips next to that bet, so that there are now two equivalent bets side by side. The dealer will then deal one card face down, usually slipping that card under the player's bet. The bettor may look at that card if he desires.

7

4—Splitting Pairs

If dealt a pair of identical value cards, such as 3-3, 7-7, 8-8 (any combination of 10, J, Q, K is considered a pair), the player can split these cards so that two separate hands are formed. To split a pair, the player turns the pair face up, separates them, putting each card in its own place in front of his bet. He then places a bet equal to the original wager behind the second hand. Each hand is played separately, using finger and hand signals to indicate hitting and standing.

If the first card dealt to either split hand has a value identical to the original split cards, that card may be split again (resplit) into a third hand, with the exception of Aces. When the player splits Aces, he can receive only one card on each Ace and may not draw again, no matter what card is drawn.

5—Doubling Down After Splitting

The player can double down on one or both of the hands resulting from a split according to the normal doubling rules of the casino. This option is offered in all Atlantic City casinos and in certain Nevada casinos.

For example, if a pair of 8s are split, and a 3 is drawn to the first 8 for an 11, the player may elect to double down on that 11. He can place an amount equal to the original bet next to the 11, and will receive only one additional card. If a 2 is drawn to the second 8, the player may double down on that hand as well.

6—Surrender (Late Surrender)

The player can give up his original two card hand and lose one half of his bet after it has been determined that the dealer does not have a blackjack. To surrender, the bettor turns both his cards face up, puts them above his bet, and says "surrender." The dealer will collect the cards and take one half of the bet. This option is offered in only a few Nevada casinos.

7—Early Surrender

A player option to give up his hand and lose half his bet before the dealer checks for a blackjack. This option originally introduced in Atlantic City is no longer offered because of recent changes in Atlantic City rules.

8—Insurance

If the dealer shows an Ace as his upcard, he will ask the players if they want insurance. If any player exercises this option, he is in effect betting that the dealer has a 10-value card as his hole card, a blackjack. To take insurance, he places up to one-half the amount of his bet in the area marked insurance. If the dealer does indeed have a blackjack, he gets paid 2 to 1 on the insurance bet, while losing the original bet. In effect, the transaction is a "standoff," and no money is lost. If the dealer does not have a blackjack, the insurance bet is lost and play continues.

If the player holds a blackjack and takes insurance on the dealer's Ace, the payoff will be even-money whether the dealer has a blackjack or not. Suppose the player has a $10 bet and takes insurance for $5 on his blackjack. If the dealer has a blackjack, the player wins 2 to 1 on his $5 insurance bet and ties with his own blackjack. If the dealer doesn't have a blackjack, the player loses the $5 insurance bet but gets paid 3 to 2 on his blackjack. Either way the bettor wins $10.

Insurance Strategy

Insurance is a bad bet for the following reason:

Making an insurance wager is betting that the dealer has a 10 under his Ace. Since the insurance payoff is 2 to 1, the wager will only be a profitable option for the player when the ratio of 10s to other cards is either equal to or less than 2 to 1.

A full deck has 36 non-tens and 16 tens, a ratio greater than 2 to 1. If the first deal off the top of the deck gives us a hand of 9, 7, and the dealer shows an Ace, then we know three cards, all non-tens. Now the ratio is 33 to 16, still greater than 2 to 1, still a poor bet. If you have two 10s for a 20, then the ratio is 35 to 14, an even worse bet.

Insuring a Blackjack

Taking insurance when you have a blackjack is also a bad bet, despite the well intentioned advice of dealers and other players to always "insure" a blackjack. When you have a blackjack, you know three cards, your 10 and Ace, and the dealer's Ace. The already poor starting ratio of thirty-six 10s to non-tens gets worse, becoming 34 to 15. Taking insurance when you have a blackjack gives the house an 8% advantage, a poor proposition for the player.

The Play of the Game

The dealer shuffles the cards and offers the cut to one of the players. If refused, it is offered to another player. The dealer completes the cut, and removes the top card, called the **burn card**. The burn card is either put under the deck face up, where all subsequent cards will be placed, or is put face down into a plastic case (procedures vary from casino to casino) to be followed similarly by future discards.

Players must make their bets before the cards are dealt.

The dealer deals clockwise from his left to his right, one card at a time, until each player and the dealer have received two cards. The players' cards are usually dealt face down, though it makes no difference if they are dealt face up as they sometimes are, for the dealer is bound by strict rules from which he cannot deviate. The dealer deals only one of his two cards face up. This card is called an **upcard**. The face down card is known as the **hole card** or the **downcard**.

If the dealer's upcard is an Ace, he will ask the players if they want insurance. Players that decide to take that option place a bet up to one-half their wager in front of their bet in the area marked insurance. If the dealer has a blackjack, all players that did not take insurance lose their original bets. Players that took insurance break even on the play. If the dealer hasn't a blackjack, he collects the lost insurance bets and play continues.

If the dealer shows a 10-value card, he must check his hole card for an Ace. If he has a blackjack, it is an automatic winner for the house. All player bets are lost. (Players can't insure against a 10-value card.) Players that hold blackjack push on the play. If the dealer doesn't have a blackjack, he will face the first player and await that player's decision.

Play begins with the bettor on the dealer's left, in the position known as **first base**.

The player has the option to stand, hit, double down, split (if he has two cards of equal value) and surrender (if allowed). If the player doesn't wish to hit his hand, he slips the cards under his bet indicating he will stand pat (not draw any cards). Otherwise he can draw cards until he is satisfied with his total or busts, or he can exercise one of the other options discussed previously.

Play then moves to the next player. If any player busts, or receives a blackjack, he must turn over his cards immediately. If a bust, the dealer will collect the lost bet. If a blackjack, the dealer will pay the player 3 to 2 on his bet.

After the last player has acted upon his cards, the dealer will turn his hole card over so that all players can view both of his cards. He must play his hand according to the strict guidelines regulating his play; drawing to 17, then standing. (In some casinos the dealer must draw to a soft 17.) If the dealer busts, all players still in the game for that round of play win automatically.

After playing his hand, the dealer will turn over each player's cards in turn, paying the winners, and collecting from the losers. Once the bettor has played his hand, he shouldn't touch his cards again. He should let the dealer expose his hand which he will do once the dealer has played out his own hand.

When the round has been completed, all players must place a new bet before the next deal.

Casino Personnel

The casino employee responsible for the running of the blackjack game is called the dealer. The dealer's duties are to deal the cards to the players, and play out his own hand according to the rules of the game. He converts money into chips for players entering the game or buying in for more chips during the course of the game, makes the correct payoffs for winning hands, and collects bets from the losers.

The dealer's supervisor—technically called the **floorman**, but more commonly referred to as the **pit boss**—is responsible for the supervision of between 4-6 tables. His job is to make sure the games run smoothly and to settle any disputes that may arise with a player. More importantly, his job is to oversee the exchange of money and to correct any errors that may occur.

Entering a Game

To enter a blackjack game, sit down at any unoccupied seat at the blackjack table, and place the money you wish to gamble with near the betting box in front of you, informing the dealer that you would like to get some chips for your cash. Chips may be purchased in various denominations. Let the dealer know which chips or combination of chips you'd like.

The dealer will take your money and call out the amount he is changing so that the pit boss is aware that a transaction is taking place, and can supervise that exchange.

Converting Traveller's Checks and Money Orders to Cash

The dealers will accept only cash or chips, so if you bring traveller's checks, money orders or the like, you must go to the area of the casino marked **Casino Cashier** to get these converted to cash. Be sure to bring proper identification to insure a smooth transaction.

Casino Chips

Standard denominations of casino chips are $1, $5, $25, $100 and for the high rollers, $500 and even $1,000 chips can sometimes be obtained. Though some casinos use their own color code, the usual color scheme of chips are: $1 = silver, $5 = red, $25 = green and $100 = black.

Betting

Casinos prefer that the player uses chips for betting purposes, for the handling of money at the tables is cumbersome and slows the game. However, cash can be used to bet with, though all pay-offs will be in chips.

To bet, place your chips (or cash) in the betting box directly in front of you. All bets must be placed before the cards are dealt.

House Limits

Placards located at either corner of the table indicate the minimum and maximum bets allowed at a particular table. Within the same casino you will find minimums ranging from $1, $2 and $5 to other tables that require the players to bet at least $25 or $100 per hand.

At the $1, $2 and $5 tables, the house maximum generally will not exceed $500 to $1,000 while the $25 and $100 tables may allow the players to bet as high as $3,000 a hand.

Converting Chips into Cash

Dealers do not convert your chips into cash. When you are ready to cash in your chips, take them to the cashier's cage where they'll be changed into cash.

Free Drinks and Cigarettes

Casinos offer their customers unlimited free drinking while playing at the table. In addition to alcoholic beverages, a player can order milk, soft drinks, juices or any other beverages. This is ordered through and served by a cocktail waitress.

Cigarettes and cigars are also complimentary and can be ordered through the cocktail waitress.

The Decks of Cards

Nevada casinos use one, two, four, six and sometimes as many as eight decks of cards in their blackjack games. Often, within the same casino, single and multiple deck games will be offered.

When one or two decks are used, the dealer holds the cards in his hand. When more than two decks are used, the cards are dealt from a rectangular plastic or wooden device known as a **shoe**. The shoe is designed to hold multiple decks of cards, and allows them to be easily removed one card at a time by the dealer.

Atlantic City casinos offer only 6 deck games.

Each deck used in blackjack is a standard pack of 52 cards, consisting of 4 cards of each value, Ace through King. Suits have no relevance in blackjack. Only the numerical value of the cards count.

Rules and Variations of the Casino Centers

The rules and variations affecting blackjack differ in each jurisdiction (Las Vegas, Northern Nevada and Atlantic City). In Nevada, they may differ from casino to casino, and often, they may vary within a particular casino.

Nevada Rules

The Las Vegas Strip rules are all advantageous to the player. The exceptions noted in Downtown Las Vegas and in Northern Nevada are slightly disadvantageous to the player.

Las Vegas Strip Rules

Dealer must draw on all totals of 16 or less, and stand on all totals of 17-21.

Player may take insurance on a dealer's Ace. Insurance payoffs are 2 to 1.

Player receives a 3 to 2 payoff on his blackjack.

Player may double down on any initial two card combination.

Identical pairs may be split, resplit, and drawn to as desired with the exception of split Aces, on which the player is allowed only one hit on each Ace.

Downtown Las Vegas.

Rules are the same as the Strip rules with one exception: Dealer must draw to soft 17.

Northern Nevada

Same as Strip rules with two exceptions:

Dealer must draw to soft 17.

Doubling is restricted to two card totals of 10 and 11 only.

The single deck Las Vegas Strip game is the most favorable for the player. The unfavorable variations of Northern Nevada and Downtown Las Vegas put the player at a slight disadvantage to the house, but this can easily be overcome by using the winning techniques presented later.

Atlantic City Rules

The New Jersey Casino Control Commission regulates the rules and variations offered in Atlantic City casinos, and all Atlantic City clubs must abide by the following guidelines:

Dealer must draw to all totals 16 or less, and stand on all totals of 17-21.

Player may take insurance on a dealer's Ace. Insurance payoffs are 2 to 1.

Player receives a 3 to 2 payoff on his blackjack.

Player may double on any initial two card combination.

Identical pairs may be split but not resplit.

Doubling after splitting allowed.

Six decks of cards are standard.

III. GENERAL STRATEGIC CONCEPTS

The Dealer's Only Advantage

Before we examine the correct strategies of play, it would be instructive to look at a losing strategy. In this strategy, the player will mimic the dealer; he'll draw on all totals 16 or less, and stand on all totals 17-21.

The player doing this figures that, since this strategy wins for the dealer, it must be effective for the player as well. After all, the dealer and the player will get the same number of good hands and the same number of poor hands. And if we draw just as the dealer draws, we must come out even, mustn't we?

No. As a matter of fact, the player will be playing at about a 5½% disadvantage to the house. The "Mimic the Dealer" strategy overlooks one important thing. The player must act upon his hand first.

The dealer's only advantage lies in the fact that once the player has busted, the player's bet is automatically lost, regardless of the outcome of the dealer's hand. While both the dealer and the player will bust equally following these drawing-to-17 guidelines (about 28% of the time), the double bust, where both the dealer and the player bust on the same round, will occur approximately 8% of the time (28% of 28% of the time or 28 x 28). And since the player acted first, this 8% of the time (the double bust) will be the house advantage.

When we adjust for the 3 to 2 bonus the player receives on blackjacks, a bonus the house does not enjoy, we find the house enjoying a 5½% edge over the player that follows the "Mimic the Dealer" strategy.

Overcoming the Disadvantage of Acting First

In the "Mimic the Dealer" strategy, we played our hands as if our goal was to get as close to 21 as reasonably possible, by using 17 as a cut-off point for drawing. But this losing strategy misstates the goal of the player. In blackjack, the object is to beat the dealer. Our chances of winning are not determined by how close our total approaches 21 as the other strategy assumed, but on how good our total is compared to the dealer's total.

We can overcome the disadvantage of having to act first by making judicious use of the options available to us as a player. Not only should we double down, split pairs, hit, stand and surrender (if allowed), but we can use our knowledge of the dealer's exposed upcard to fully capitalize on these options. Needless to say, adjusting our strategy according to this knowledge of the dealer's upcard will vastly improve on the "Get as Close to 21—Mimic the Dealer" strategy, and completely eliminate the house edge.

To Beat the Dealer

There are two factors that affect our chances of winning; the strength of our total and the strength of the dealer's total. To beat the dealer, we must know how strong our total is compared to the dealer's total so that we know if drawing additional cards or exercising a player option is a viable consideration. In addition, we must be aware of the factors that influence the final outcome of these totals so that we can determine the optimal way to play our hand.

In determining the best way to play our hand, we must know how good our total is as it stands. Do we have the expectancy of winning by standing? If so, can we increase this expectancy by drawing additional cards or by exercising a doubling or splitting option when applicable? If we do not have the expectancy of winning by standing, will the drawing of additional cards or the employment of the doubling or splitting option increase our chance of winning?

Since our object is to beat the dealer, to answer the question "how strong is our total?" we need to ask ourselves if the dealer's expectancy, judged by the information we get from his exposed card is greater than our total. Being able to see the dealer's upcard gives us a great deal of information about the strength of the hands that the dealer is likely to make, and we can use that information to our advantage.

Understanding the Dealer's Upcard

Being able to see the dealer's upcard is of great value to the player, for there are two factors—the rules governing the dealer's play of his hand, and the number of tens in a deck of cards (ten factor)—that tell us a great deal about the potential strength of the dealer's hands, and the frequency with which those hands will bust.

Ten Factor

The most striking feature of blackjack is the dominant role that the 10 value cards (10, J, Q, K) play. Each ten and face card is counted as 10 points each in blackjack, and the player is four times more likely to draw a 10 than any other individual card since all the other value cards, Aces through nines, consist of only four cards each as opposed to sixteen 10s. Collectively, the 10s constitute just under 1/3 of the deck (16 out of 52 cards).

Because the 10s are such a dominant factor in a deck of cards, it's correct to think of the dealer's hand gravitating toward a total 10 points greater than his exposed upcard. When I speak of a hand as gravitating toward a total, I am referring to the tendency of that hand to increase in value by 10 points as a result of the 10 factor. Thus, starting out with an upcard of 9, the dealer will make a hand of 19 thirty-six percent of the time and 19 or better 52% of the time.

The Dealer's Rules and the Ten Factor

Our strategy is based on the fact that the dealer must play by prescribed guidelines from which he cannot deviate. He must draw to all totals 16 or below, and stand on all totals 17-21 (except in casinos that require the dealer to draw to soft 17). All hard totals that exceed hard 21 are automatic dealer losses.

By combining our knowledge of the 10 factor with the above-mentioned dealer rules gives us a natural separation of the dealer's upcard into two distinct groupings: 2s through 6s, the dealer's "stiff" cards, and 7s through As (Aces), the dealer's "pat" cards.

2s through 6s—Dealer Stiff Cards

Whenever the dealer shows a 2, 3, 4, 5 or 6 as an upcard, we know that he must draw at least one additional card regardless of the value of his hole card (unless the dealer has an Ace under his Six and is playing Las Vegas Strip or Atlantic City rules which require the dealer to stand on soft 17). The high concentration of 10s in the deck make it likely that the dealer will expose a 10 as his hole card, giving him a stiff total of 12-16.

Since the dealer must draw to all hard totals 16 or below, the drawing of a 10 (and in some instances, smaller totalled cards) will bust any of these stiff totals. For example, if the dealer shows a 6, and reveals a 10 in the hole, any card higher than a 5 will bust his hand.

Thus, the high concentration of 10s in the deck tell us that the dealer has a good chance of busting when his upcard is a 2, 3, 4, 5 or 6.

7s through As—Dealer Pat Cards

Whenever the dealer shows a 7, 8, 9, 10 or A as an upcard, we know, because of the large number of 10s, that he has a high likelihood of making pat totals 17-21, and conversely, a smaller chance of busting than when he shows a stiff card. This high concentration of 10s makes it likely that the dealer will expose a 10 for an automatic pat hand (17-21). Even when he hasn't a 10 in the hole, combinations such as 8, 9; A, 7; 9, 9 and so forth, give him an automatic pat hand as well.

Chart 1
Understanding the Dealer's Upcard

Dealer Stiff Cards—Advantageous for Player

2	3		4	5	6
Less Advantageous			**More Advantageous**		

2 and 3—Though it is favorable for the player when the dealer shows a 2 or a 3 as an upcard, we will need to be cautious against these stiff cards, for the dealer will bust less often with these than when he shows the 4, 5 and 6.

4, 5 and 6—The dealer is showing the upcards you always want him to hold. The dealer will bust about 42% of the time with these upcards (5% more than the 2, 3 and about 18% more than with the pat cards). We will take advantage of these weak dealer upcards by aggressive splitting and doubling.

Dealer Pat Cards—Disadvantageous for Player

7	8	9		10	Ace
Moderately Disadvantageous				**Very Disadvantageous**	

7 and 8—While the dealer will not bust often with these upcards, they also indicate to us that the dealer's hands gravitate toward the weaker totals of 17 and 18. It is interesting to note that of all the dealer upcards including the stiff cards, the 7 will form the weakest totals.

9, 10 and Ace—The 9 and 10 gravitate toward totals of 19 and 20 respectively—tough hands to beat. The Ace is also a powerful dealer upcard, for in addition to forming strong hands, the dealer will bust less with an Ace than with any other upcard.

Against these powerful upcards, we will be very cautious in our doubling and splitting strategies.

Understanding the Player's Hand—Hard Totals

The player's totals can be divided into three distinct groupings: 11 or less, 17-21 and 12-16. We will look at each in turn to see how they affect our strategy.

11 or Less—(Hard Totals)

We should always draw to any hard total 11 or less (unless a doubling or splitting option is more profitable). By hitting this hand we have no risk of busting, no matter what we draw, and the drawing of a card can strengthen our total. There is no question about the correct decision; drawing is a big gain.

17-21—(Hard Totals)

We should always stand on these hard totals (17-21), for the risk of busting is too high to make drawing worthwhile. It should be obvious that the chances of improving these high totals are minimal, and the risks of busting very probable. In addition, totals of 19, 20, 21 and, to a lesser extent, 18 are already powerful hands. While hard 17 is a poor player total, the risk of busting by drawing is way too costly to make drawing a viable option. Stand on hard totals of 17-21 against any dealer's upcard.

12-16—(Hard Totals)

With these hands the bulk of our decision making will be exercised, for on these hard totals there are no automatic decisions as on the other player totals. Our hand is not an obvious draw (such as the 11 or less grouping) for the risk of drawing a 10 or other high card and busting is substantial. Our hand is not an obvious stand decision either (such as the 17-21 grouping), for the only times we will win with these weak totals of 12-16 are the times that the dealer busts.

For the Cardoza Non-Counter winning strategies to be effective, you must first know the correct way to play your hands. Therefore, make sure you understand these basic strategies before going on to the winning techniques of play.

IV. THE OPTIMAL BASIC STRATEGIES

Hitting and Standing—Hard Totals

These strategies are applicable for single and multiple deck games in all casino centers.

General Principles—

1. When the dealer shows a 7, 8, 9, 10 or A, hit all hard totals of 16 or below.

2. When the dealer shows a 2, 3, 4, 5 or 6, stand on all hard totals of 12 or more. Do not bust against a dealer stiff card. Exception– Hit 12 vs. 2, 3.

Chart 2
Hitting and Standing—Hard Totals
All Casino Centers

	2	3	4	5	6	7	8	9	10	A
11 or less	H	H	H	H	H	H	H	H	H	H
12	H	H	S	S	S	H	H	H	H	H
13	S	S	S	S	S	H	H	H	H	H
14	S	S	S	S	S	H	H	H	H	H
15	S	S	S	S	S	H	H	H	H	H
16	S	S	S	S	S	H	H	H	H	H
17-21	S	S	S	S	S	S	S	S	S	S

H = Hit   S = Stand

(The dealer's upcard is indicated by the horizontal numbers and the player's hand is indicated by the vertical numbers. The letters in the matrix indicate the correct strategy play.)

Conceptual Hitting and Standing Strategy

In the "Understanding the Player's Hand" section we discussed our strategy for hard totals of 11 or less, and for hard totals 17-21. They will be reiterated briefly here.

11 or less—Draw against all dealer upcards.
17-21—Stand against all dealer upcards.

Hard Totals 12-16

It is when we hold hard totals 12-16 (stiffs) that the player's big disadvantage of having to go first (the only built-in house advantage) is a costly proposition. If we draw to hard totals and bust, we are automatic losers. But, on the other hand, if we stand, we will win with these weak totals only when the dealer busts.

It is important to realize that the decision to hit or stand with hard totals 12-16 is a strategy of minimizing losses, for no matter what we do, we have a potentially losing hand against any dealer upcard. Do not expect to win when you hold a stiff. However, in order to maximize the gain from our overall strategy, we must minimize the losses in disadvantageous situations (as above), and maximize our gains in advantageous ones.

a. Player Totals of 12-16 vs. Dealer Pat Cards 7, 8, 9, 10, A

When the dealer's upcard is a 7 through an Ace, you should expect the dealer to make his hand, for he will bust only about one time in four, a mere 25% of the time. If we stand on our hard totals 12-16, we will win only the times that the dealer busts.

Thus, for every 100 hands that we stand with our stiff totals 12-16 against dealer pat cards, our expectation is to lose 75 of those hands and to win only 25, a net loss of 50 hands. Not an exciting prognosis.

On the other hand, drawing to our stiff totals 12-16 against the dealer pat cards gives us a big gain over standing. By drawing, we will gain an average of 15%. The dealer makes too many hands showing a 7, 8, 9, 10 or Ace, to allow us to stand with our stiffs.

You will bust often when drawing to your stiffs, but do not let that dissuade you from hitting your stiffs against pat cards. The strategy on these plays is to minimize losses. We cannot afford to stand and sacrifice our hand to the 3 out of 4 hands that the dealer will make.

When the dealer shows a 7, 8, 9, 10, or Ace, hit all hard totals 16 or below.

b. Player Totals of 12-16 vs. Dealer Pat Cards 2, 3, 4, 5, 6

The greater busting potential of the dealer stiff cards makes standing with hard player totals of 12-16 a big gain over drawing. While we will win only 40% of these hands (the times that the dealer busts), standing is a far superior strategy to drawing, for we will bust too often drawing to our own stiffs against upcards that will bust fairly often themselves. The times that we would make pat totals by drawing wouldn't guarantee us winners either, for the dealer will often make equal or better totals.

On these plays, our disadvantage of having to go first makes drawing too costly, for once we bust, we automatically lose. Though the dealer will make more hands than bust, our strategy here is to minimize losses so that when we get our good hands, we'll come out an overall winner.

Exception—Hit Player 12 vs. 2, 3

Hitting 12 vs. 2, 3 is the only basic strategy exception to drawing with a stiff total against a dealer's stiff upcard. The double bust factor is not as costly on these plays, for only the 10s will bust our 12. Similarly, the dealer will bust less often showing a 2 or a 3 than with the other stiff cards, 4, 5 and 6.*

The combination of the player being less likely to bust (more likely to make his hand) and the dealer being more likely to make his hand (less likely to bust) makes drawing a player 12 vs. 2, 3 the correct strategy play.

Hitting and Standing—Soft Totals

The strategy for hitting and standing with soft totals in Northern Nevada is identical to the Atlantic City and Las Vegas strategies for both single and multiple deck, except that the Atlantic City and Las Vegas basic strategy players can take advantage of the more liberal doubling rules and will double down on hands that the Northern Nevada player cannot.

*This is in contrast to the play 13 vs. 2 where the correct strategy is to stand. The additional player busting factor of the 9 makes the player slightly better off by standing, even though the dealer will bust less with a 2 as an upcard. This clearly illustrates the greater importance of the player's busting factor (compared to the dealer's busting factor) when deciding whether to stand or draw with a stiff total 12-16 vs. a dealer stiff upcard.

21

Chart 3
Hitting and Standing—Soft Totals
Northern Nevada—Single and Multiple Deck

	2	3	4	5	6	7	8	9	10	A
A2-A6	H	H	H	H	H	H	H	H	H	H
A7	S	S	S	S	S	S	S	H	H	H
A8-A9	S	S	S	S	S	S	S	S	S	S

H = Hit   S = Stand

Chart 4
Hitting and Standing—Soft Totals
Atlantic City, Las Vegas—Single and Multiple Deck

	2	3	4	5	6	7	8	9	10	A
A2-A5	H	H	D*	D	D	H	H	H	H	H
A6	D*	D	D	D	D	H	H	H	H	H
A7	S	D	D	D	D	S	S	H	H	H
A8	S	S	S	S	S	S	S	S	S	S
A9	S	S	S	S	S	S	S	S	S	S

H = Hit   S = Stand   D = Double

(For discussion of Atlantic City and Las Vegas Doubling Strategies, see Doubling Section)

*Note multiple deck exceptions in doubling section.

Conceptual Hitting and Standing—Soft Totals
A2, A3, A4, A5

Unless the player is able to double down, he should always draw a card to these hands. Standing is a poor option, for these totals will win only when the dealer busts. The player has nothing to lose by drawing (no draw can bust these totals), and may improve his total. Players that stand on these hands might just as well give the casinos their money. Draw on A2-A5 against all dealer upcards.

A6, A7, A8, A9

The decision to hit or stand with soft totals 17 or more necessitates a closer look at the strength of these totals. Unlike hard totals of 17 or more, drawing is a viable option with these soft totals. Since we have the option of counting the Ace as 1 point or 11 points, the drawing of a 10 or, for that matter, the drawing of any other card, will not bust our soft totals. While we have no risk of busting, we do have the risk of drawing a weaker total, and therefore must ask the question, "How strong is our total?"

For soft totals, we want to know:

1—What are our chances of winning by standing?

2—What are the chances of improving our hand by drawing additional cards?

Soft 17 (A6)

A standing total of 17 is a weak hand against all dealer upcards, including the dealer stiff cards, and in the long run is a losing total. The only time we will win with this total is when the dealer busts. Otherwise, at best we have a push.

Always draw on soft 17 no matter what the dealer shows as an upcard. (In Las Vegas and Atlantic City, the correct strategy may be to double down. See doubling section.) This standing total is so weak that attempting to improve our hand by drawing is always a tremendous gain against any upcard.

When a casino requires the dealer to draw to soft 17, it is a disadvantageous rule to the player. Though the dealer will sometimes bust by drawing to a soft 17, in the long run he will make more powerful totals, and have more winners. It affects the player the same way.

Soft 18

Against dealer stiff totals of 2, 3, 4, 5 and 6, standing with our 18 is a smart strategy move (unless playing Las Vegas or Atlantic City doubling rules where doubling will often be a big player gain). We have a strong total against these weak dealer upcards.

Stand against dealer upcards of 7 and 8, for our 18 is a solid hand. Against the 7, we have a winning total, and against the 8, we figure to have a potential push, as these dealer upcards gravitate toward 17 and 18 respectively. We do not want to risk our strong position by drawing.

Against the powerful dealer upcards of 9, 10, Ace, our standing total of 18 is a potentially losing hand. Normally you would think that hitting a soft 18 is only a fair total. We are not chancing a powerful total but rather attempting to improve a weak situation.

As a matter of fact, for every 100 plays (at $1 a play) that we draw rather than stand on soft 18 vs. 9 and 10, we will gain $9 and $4 respectively. You must realize that 18 vs. 9, 10, Ace is not a winning hand and since our 18 is a soft total, we have a chance to minimize losses by drawing.

Soft 19 and 20

These hands are strong player totals as they stand. We have no need of improving these already powerful totals.

Doubling Down

Doubling down is a valuable option for it gives the player a chance to double his bet in advantageous situations. The only drawback to the doubling option is that the player receives one card and gives up the privilege to draw additional cards should that card be a poor draw. To determine if the doubling option will be profitable, we must weigh the benefits of doubling our bet against the drawbacks of receiving only one card.

One of the most important factors to consider when contemplating the doubling option is the 10 factor. We are more likely to draw a 10 on our double than any other card value. Thus, doubling on a total of 11, where the drawing of a 10 gives us an unbeatable 21, is a more powerful double than an initial two card total of 9, where the drawing of a 10 gives us a strong total of 19, not as powerful as the 21.

On the other hand, we would not double any hand of hard 12 or more, for the drawing of a 10 would bust our total, and we would have an automatic loser at double the bet.

The 10 factor is also an important strategic consideration, for it affects the dealer's busting potential. We double more aggressively against the weakest of the dealer stiff cards, the 4, 5 and 6, and less aggressively against the other stiff cards, the 2 and 3. The only times we will double against the dealer pat cards are when our doubling totals 10 and 11, are powerful themselves.

Doubling Down
Single Deck Basic Strategy

A. Northern Nevada—The player is restricted to doubling down on two card totals of 10 and 11 only.

Chart 5
Doubling Down
Northern Nevada—Single Deck

	2	3	4	5	6	7	8	9	10	A
10	D	D	D	D	D	D	D	D		
11	D	D	D	D	D	D	D	D	D	D

D = Double Down   **Blank** = Do Not Double Down

B. Las Vegas—The player can double down on any initial two card combination.

Chart 6
Doubling Down
Las Vegas Single Deck

	2	3	4	5	6	7	8	9	10	A
62										
44, 53				D	D					
9	D	D	D	D	D					
10	D	D	D	D	D	D	D	D		
11	D	D	D	D	D	D	D	D	D	D
A2				D	D	D				
A3				D	D	D				
A4				D	D	D				
A5				D	D	D				
A6	D	D	D	D	D					
A7		D	D	D	D					
A8										
A9										

D = Double Down   **Blank** = Do Not Double Down

Multiple Deck Basic Strategy

A. Northern Nevada—The player is restricted to doubling down on two card totals of 10 and 11 only.

Chart 7
Doubling Down
Northern Nevada—Multiple Deck

	2	3	4	5	6	7	8	9	10	A
10	D	D	D	D	D	D	D	D		
11	D	D	D	D	D	D	D	D	D	

D = Double Down   Blank = Do Not Double Down

B. The player can double down on any initial two card combination. These strategies are good for all multiple deck games in Atlantic City and Las Vegas.

Chart 8
Doubling Down
Atlantic City, Las Vegas—Multiple Deck

	2	3	4	5	6	7	8	9	10	A
8										
9		D	D	D	D					
10	D	D	D	D	D	D	D	D		
11	D	D	D	D	D	D	D	D	D	
A2				D	D					
A3				D	D					
A4			D	D	D					
A5			D	D	D					
A6		D	D	D	D					
A7		D	D	D	D					
A8										
A9										

D = Double Down   Blank = Do Not Double Down

Conceptual Doubling—Hard Totals (11, 10, 9, 8)

These strategies are applicable to single and multiple deck games in all casino centers. Where multiple deck strategies differ from the single deck, an asterisk will denote the strategy change, and that change will be indicated.

11*

This is the strongest doubling hand for the player and should be doubled against all the dealer upcards in a single deck game. If we draw a 10 value card on our double, we will have a 21, the strongest hand we can have. At best, the dealer can tie us.

*Do not double 11 vs. Ace in multiple deck games.

10

This is the second strongest doubling hand for the player and should be doubled against the dealer's 2 through 9. Our hard 10 gravitates toward a 20, an overwhelmingly strong hand against these dealer upcards.

Do not double 10 against the dealer's 10 or Ace. Doubling our hard 10 against the dealer's 10 is not a potential winner as before (against the dealer's 2 through 9), for the dealer's hand gravitates toward a 20 as well, and our possible 20 is not powerful enough to compensate for the low busting probabilities of the dealer's Ace. Giving up the option to draw an additional card should the first card be a poor one is too costly on these plays.

Note: In Northern Nevada, only hard 10 and 11 can be doubled down.

9

Double 9 against 2 through 6 only.* The high busting potential of the dealer stiff cards (2-6) makes the 9 a profitable double down. We cannot double down against any of the pat cards (7-Ace) for our win potential when we do draw the 10 (for a total of 19) is not strong enough to compensate for the times when we draw a poor card and cannot draw again.

*Do not double 9 vs. 2 in a multiple deck game.

8

Doubling 8 vs. 5, 6 is a valid play in a single deck game*. Our 8 gravitates toward an 18, only a fair total. However, the very high busting potential of the dealer 5 and 6 make this double a slight gain. Our 8 is not strong enough to make doubling against the other dealer upcards a good play.

*Do not double 8 against any upcard in a multiple deck game.

Conceptual Doubling—Soft Totals

The high concentration of 10s play a different role in soft doubling than in hard doubling, for instead of having a positive effect on our chances of making a good total, the drawing of a 10 will not even give us a pat hand on many of these doubles.

Doubling with our soft totals is generally a gain against the weak dealer upcards, for the 10 factor will figure strongly in the dealer's chances of busting, while the drawing of small and medium cards will often improve our hand to a competitive total.

A2, A3, A4, A5

Double A2, A3, A4 and A5 against the dealer's 4, 5 and 6*. The very high busting probabilities of the dealer 4, 5 and 6 makes doubling with our A2 to A5 profitable for the player. Again, the drawing of a 10 value card does not help our total, but the high dealer busting factor gives us an edge.

We do not double against the 2 and 3, because the dealer will make just too many hands with these upcards. The same is more strikingly true with the dealer pat cards, 7 through Ace.

*Do not double A2 vs. 4 and A3 vs. 4 in a multiple deck game.

A6

Double A6 vs. dealer 2, 3, 4, 5 and 6*. The A6 is a more powerful double than the A2-A5, for the drawing of a 10 to the A6 will at least give us a pat total and a potential push against a dealer's 17. This "push" factor enables us to gain by doubling against the dealer's 2 and 3 despite the fact that they will make more dealer pat totals than with the weaker upcards 4, 5 and 6.

*Do not double A6 vs. 2 in a multiple deck game.

A7

Double A7 vs. 3, 4, 5 and 6. Our soft 18 is only a fair total and drawing an additional card won't risk the destruction of a powerful total such as a 19 or 20.

Soft 18 is a strong double against the weaker dealer stiffs 4, 5 and 6, but differs from the soft 17 in that we do not double against the 2. A standing total of 18 vs. a 2 is a stronger winning hand and we do not want to risk the weakening of this hand by doubling and having to draw a card.

A8, A9

We have two very strong totals here and do not want to risk our excellent chances of winning by attempting to double.

Splitting Pairs

Splitting can do two valuable things. It can turn one poor total into two stronger hands (such as splitting a hard 16 (8-8) into two hands of 8 each) and it effectively doubles our bet.

The decision to split requires a closer look at our hand vs. the dealer's hand, for we must balance the standing total of our hand against the two proposed split hands, and see if the split and resultant doubling of our bet increases our expectation of winning.

Here's our thought process:

1—How strong is our total as it stands.

Is the hand too powerful a total as it stands to risk breaking up? If not, we can consider the split.

2—How strong are the two proposed split totals?

Thinking in terms of the 10 factor, we want to see if our split totals gravitate toward strong totals relative to the strength of the dealer's upcard, or if the split totals represent an improvement over the hard standing original hand.

And finally,

3—Does splitting either increase our chances of winning or reduce our rate of loss?

These factors are our guides in seeing if a split produces a gain for us.

Single Deck Basic Strategy

These strategies are applicable to all Northern Nevada and Las Vegas single deck games.

Chart 9
Splitting Pairs
Northern Nevada, Las Vegas—Single Deck

	2	3	4	5	6	7	8	9	10	A
22		Spl.	Spl.	Spl.	Spl.	Spl.				
33			Spl.	Spl.	Spl.	Spl.				
66	Spl.	Spl.	Spl.	Spl.	Spl.					
77	Spl.	Spl.	Spl.	Spl.	Spl.	Spl.				
88	Spl.	Spl.	Spl.	Spl.	Spl.	Spl.	Spl.	Spl.	Spl.	Spl.
99	Spl.	Spl.	Spl.	Spl.	Spl.		Spl.	Spl.		
AA	Spl.	Spl.	Spl.	Spl.	Spl.	Spl.	Spl.	Spl.	Spl.	Spl.

Spl. = Split   Blank = Do Not Split

Do not split 44, 55, 10s
Always split 88, AA

Multiple Deck Basic Strategy
A. Las Vegas and Northern Nevada Multiple Deck.

Chart 10
Splitting Pairs
Northern Nevada, Las Vegas—Multiple Deck

	2	3	4	5	6	7	8	9	10	A
22			Spl.	Spl.	Spl.	Spl.				
33			Spl.	Spl.	Spl.	Spl.				
66		Spl.	Spl.	Spl.	Spl.					
77	Spl.	Spl.	Spl.	Spl.	Spl.	Spl.				
88	Spl.	Spl.	Spl.	Spl.	Spl.	Spl.	Spl.	Spl.	Spl.	Spl.
99	Spl.	Spl.	Spl.	Spl.	Spl.		Spl.	Spl.		
AA	Spl.	Spl.	Spl.	Spl.	Spl.	Spl.	Spl.	Spl.	Spl.	Spl.

Spl. = Split   Blank = Do Not Split

Do not split 44, 55, 10s
Always split 88, AA

B. Atlantic City (and selected Nevada casinos where doubling down after splitting is permitted)—Because of the doubling after splitting rule, the player will split pairs more aggressively, so that he can take advantage of good doubling situations that may arise as a consequences of the split.

Chart 11
Splitting Pairs
Atlantic City

	2	3	4	5	6	7	8	9	10	A
22	Spl.	Spl.	Spl.	Spl.	Spl.	Spl.				
33	Spl.	Spl.	Spl.	Spl.	Spl.	Spl.				
44				Spl.	Spl.					
66	Spl.	Spl.	Spl.	Spl.	Spl.					
77	Spl.	Spl.	Spl.	Spl.	Spl.	Spl.				
88	Spl.	Spl.	Spl.	Spl.	Spl.	Spl.	Spl.	Spl.	Spl.	Spl.
99	Spl.	Spl.	Spl.	Spl.	Spl.		Spl.	Spl.		
AA	Spl.	Spl.	Spl.	Spl.	Spl.	Spl.	Spl.	Spl.	Spl.	Spl.

Spl. = Split   Blank = Do Not Split

Do not split 55, 10s
Always split 88, AA

Conceptual Splitting

We will examine the decision to split 99 first, for it is a good example of the thinking process involved in splitting. First of all, we should note that this hand totaling 18 is only "fair," not a powerful one like a 19 or 20.

Splitting 9s
Dealer shows a 2, 3, 4, 5, 6

Split 99 against these dealer stiff cards. Our 18 is a winner, but splitting the hand into two hands of 9 each is a big gain. Each starting hand of 9, because of the 10 factor, gravitates toward strong player totals of 19. The high busting potential of the dealer stiff cards gives us an excellent opportunity to maximize our gain in an advantageous situation.

Dealer shows a 7

Stand with 99 vs. dealer 7. We figure the dealer for a 17. Our standing total of 18 is a stronger total and a big potential winner. While splitting the 9s will also produce a positive expectation of winning, the risking of our fairly secure 18 against the 7 win for two strong but chancy totals will reduce the gain. We have the dealer beat. Stand.

Dealer shows an 8

Splitting 99 against the dealer's 8 is a big gain. Against the dealer's 8, we figure our 18 to be a potential push. However, by splitting the 18 into two separate hands of 9 each, we hope to turn our potential push into two possible winners. (Each 9 gravitates toward a total of 19, one point higher than the dealer's 18).

Dealer shows a 9

Splitting 99 vs. the dealer's 9 is also a big gain. Against the 9, our 18 is a losing total, but splitting the 18 into two totals of 9 each reduces our potential loss. Rather than one losing total of 18, we will have two hands gravitating toward potential pushes.

Dealer shows a 10 or Ace

Do not split 99 against the dealer's 10 or Ace. Our split hands of 9 each gravitate toward good totals, but against these more powerful dealer upcards, splitting would be a poor play. We do not want to make one loser into two.

Splitting 22 and 33

Split 22 vs. dealer 3 through 7*.
Split 33 vs. dealer 4 through 7*.

The high busting probabilities of the dealer 4, 5 and 6 makes the 22 and 33 good splits. We split 22 vs. 3 and not 33 vs. 3, because of the lower player busting factor of our split hands of 2 each. The drawing of a 10 gives us another chance to improve on our 2, for correct basic strategy is to draw 12 vs. 3, while the drawing of a 10 on our 3 forces us to stand.

We do not split 22 or 33 vs. the dealer's 2, because the dealer's 2 does not bust often enough to make splitting a profitable play.

Splitting 22 and 33 vs. 7 seems unusual at first, for this play seems to exceed our normal strategic boundaries of making aggressive plays against the weak dealer stiff cards. Though the 7 is a pat card and will make a lot of pat hands, the 7 will also make the weakest totals, only gravitating toward a total of 17. Our starting totals of 2 and 3 will make hands of 18 or better about one-half the time. Splitting 22 and 33 against the dealer's 7 will not make us money (because of the high busting factor of our hands), but they will produce a moderate gain over drawing to these hands.

Do not split 22 and 33 against the 8, 9, 10 or Ace. We do not want to make one loser into two losers.

*Nevada multiple deck exception—Do not split 22 vs. 3.

*Atlantic City multiple deck exception—Split 22 and 33 vs. 2 through 7.

Splitting 4s

Do not split 44*. The hard total of 8 gravitates toward a total of 18, a far better position than two weak starting totals of 4 each. Against the dealer stiff cards, 2 through 6, we have a big gain by drawing to our 8. While the drawing of a 10 will not give us an overwhelmingly strong total, an 18 is far better than drawing the same 10 to a split 4. We do not want to hold two weak hands of 4 each against the dealer pat cards, especially the dealer's 7 and 8, where we have a good starting total of 8.

*Atlantic City exception—Split 44 vs. 5 and 6.

Splitting 55

Never split 55. 55 by itself is an excellent starting total of 10. You do not want to break up this powerful player total into two terrible hands of 5 each. (Our 10 is an excellent doubling hand against dealer upcards of 2 through 9.)

Splitting 66

Split 66 against dealer stiff cards 2 through 6 only.* Our hard total of 12 is not very favorable, nor are the split hands of 6 and 6 too promising either. We have a losing hand either way against all dealer upcards. However, we want to minimize our losses.

Against the dealer stiff cards 2, 3, 4, 5 and 6, our split hands of 6 and 6 will sometimes draw cards to give us some pat totals 17-21. Of course, we will often end up with stiff totals on the split pair (by the drawing of a 10 or other sufficiently large card) and be forced to stand. But the high dealer busting factor makes splitting 66 against the dealer stiffs a slight gain.

Obviously we will not split 66 against the dealer pat cards. We don't need two hands of 16 against a card that will bust only one time in four.

*Nevada multiple deck exception—Do not split 66 vs. 2.

*Atlantic City multiple deck—No exceptions. Split 66 vs. 2-6.

33

Splitting 77

Split 77 against dealer upcards of 2, 3, 4, 5, 6 and 7. Against the dealer stiff cards 2 through 6, two playable hands of 7 and 7 are preferable to one stiff total of 14. Splitting 77 is not a strong split, for these totals only gravitate toward a 17, but the high busting rate of the dealer stiff cards makes this split a big gain.

Splitting 77 against the dealer's 7 is also an excellent split, for we are taking one losing total of 14 into two potential pushes of 17 each.

We do not split 77 vs. the dealer's 8, 9, 10, Ace, for we do not want to take one poor total of 14 into two hands gravitating toward a second best total of only 17.

Splitting 88

Split 88 against all dealer upcards. Against the dealer's 2 through 8, we are taking one terrible hand of 16 into two playable totals of 8 each. There is a tremendous gain on all these plays.

Splitting 88 against the dealer's 9, 10, A are the strangest of the basic strategy plays. Using all of the intuitive knowledge we have developed, at first glance we would reason that this is a poor split, for we are making two losers out of one. However, more is involved in this play.

First, you must realize that the player hand of 16 is the worst total we can get. While splitting this 16 into two hands of 8 and 8 is not a winning situation against the strong dealer upcards of 9, 10 and A, it is an improvement over our very weak total of hard 16. Bear with this unusual play, for computer simulation studies have played out the hand millions of times for both drawing and splitting, and found that the player loses less by splitting 88. Realize that although the split is weak, it does produce a gain over drawing to our easily bustable hard 16.

Splitting 10, 10

Do not split 10s. the hard total of 20 is a winning hand against all dealer upcards. Splitting 10s against any dealer upcard is a terrible play, for you are taking one "solid" winning hand into two good but uncertain wins. Too often, the splitting of 10s will draw low cards, in effect destroying a great hand.

Splitting AA

Split AA gainst all dealer upcards. Each Ace is a powerful starting total of 11 points. If we draw the 10, our 21 can't be beat. Splitting AA is a tremendous gain against all dealer upcards.

Chart 12
Master Chart
Northern Nevada Single Deck

	2	3	4	5	6	7	8	9	10	A
8	H	H	H	H	H	H	H	H	H	H
9	H	H	H	H	H	H	H	H	H	H
10	D	D	D	D	D	D	D	D	H	H
11	D	D	D	D	D	D	D	D	D	D
12	H	H	S	S	S	H	H	H	H	H
13	S	S	S	S	S	H	H	H	H	H
14	S	S	S	S	S	H	H	H	H	H
15	S	S	S	S	S	H	H	H	H	H
16	S	S	S	S	S	H	H	H	H	H
A2	H	H	H	H	H	H	H	H	H	H
A3	H	H	H	H	H	H	H	H	H	H
A4	H	H	H	H	H	H	H	H	H	H
A5	H	H	H	H	H	H	H	H	H	H
A6	H	H	H	H	H	H	H	H	H	H
A7	S	S	S	S	S	S	S	H	H	H
A8	S	S	S	S	S	S	S	S	S	S
A9	S	S	S	S	S	S	S	S	S	S
22	H	Spl.	Spl.	Spl.	Spl.	Spl.	H	H	H	H
33	H	H	Spl.	Spl.	Spl.	Spl.	H	H	H	H
66	Spl.	Spl.	Spl.	Spl.	Spl.	H	H	H	H	H
77	Spl.	Spl.	Spl.	Spl.	Spl.	Spl.	H	H	H	H
88	Spl.	Spl.	Spl.	Spl.	Spl.	Spl.	Spl.	Spl.	Spl.	Spl.
99	Spl.	Spl.	Spl.	Spl.	Spl.	S	Spl.	Spl.	S	S
AA	Spl.	Spl.	Spl.	Spl.	Spl.	Spl.	Spl.	Spl.	Spl.	Spl.

H = Hit   **S** = Stand   **D** = Double   **Spl.** = Split

Chart 13
Master Chart
Las Vegas Single Deck

	2	3	4	5	6	7	8	9	10	A
62	H	H	H	H	H	H	H	H	H	H
44, 53	H	H	H	D	D	H	H	H	H	H
9	D	D	D	D	D	H	H	H	H	H
10	D	D	D	D	D	D	D	D	H	H
11	D	D	D	D	D	D	D	D	D	D
12	H	H	S	S	S	H	H	H	H	H
13	S	S	S	S	S	H	H	H	H	H
14	S	S	S	S	S	H	H	H	H	H
15	S	S	S	S	S	H	H	H	H	H
16	S	S	S	S	S	H	H	H	H	H
A2	H	H	D	D	D	H	H	H	H	H
A3	H	H	D	D	D	H	H	H	H	H
A4	H	H	D	D	D	H	H	H	H	H
A5	H	H	D	D	D	H	H	H	H	H
A6	D	D	D	D	D	H	H	H	H	H
A7	S	D	D	D	D	S	S	H	H	H
A8	S	S	S	S	S	S	S	S	S	S
A9	S	S	S	S	S	S	S	S	S	S
22	H	Spl.	Spl.	Spl.	Spl.	Spl.	H	H	H	H
33	H	H	Spl.	Spl.	Spl.	Spl.	H	H	H	H
66	Spl.	Spl.	Spl.	Spl.	Spl.	H	H	H	H	H
77	Spl.	Spl.	Spl.	Spl.	Spl.	Spl.	H	H	H	H
88	Spl.	Spl.	Spl.	Spl.	Spl.	Spl.	Spl.	Spl.	Spl.	Spl.
99	Spl.	Spl.	Spl.	Spl.	Spl.	S	Spl.	Spl.	S	S
AA	Spl.	Spl.	Spl.	Spl.	Spl.	Spl.	Spl.	Spl.	Spl.	Spl.

H = Hit   **S** = Stand   **D** = Double   **Spl.** = Split

Multiple Deck Basic Strategy

The greater number of cards used in a multiple deck game makes the removal of particular cards less important for composition change purposes and, as a result, our doubling and splitting strategies are less aggressive.

For example, the removal of three cards (5, 3, 5) creates a favorable imbalance for the player in a single deck game and makes a 53 double vs. the dealer's 5 a profitable play. Not only will these cards be poor draws for the player's double but they're three cards the dealer needs to improve his hand. The effective removal of these three cards gives the player a better chance of drawing a 10 on his 8 and, at the same time, increases the dealer's chance of busting. In a single deck game, 53 vs. 8 is a favorable double.

However, the removal of these three cards are barely felt in a multiple deck game. There are twenty nine other 3s and 5s in a four deck game as compared to only five in a single deck. Thus, no favorable imbalance has been created in the multiple deck game, and the double down is not a correct play.

This lack of sensitivity to particular card removal accounts for nine strategy changes in the multiple deck game. Except for the following nine changes in the doubling and splitting strategies, multiple deck basic strategy is identical to the single deck basic strategy.

1—Do not double hard 8 vs. 5; hit instead.
2—Do not double hard 8 vs. 6; hit instead.
3—Do not double hard 9 vs. 2; hit instead.
4—Do not double hard 11 vs. Ace; hit instead.
5—Do not double A2 vs. 4; hit instead.
6—Do not double A3 vs. 4; hit instead.
7—Do not double A6 vs. 2; hit instead.
8—Do not split 22 vs. 3; hit instead.
9—Do not split 66 vs. 2; hit instead.

Chart 14
Master Chart
Northern Nevada Multiple Deck

	2	3	4	5	6	7	8	9	10	A
8	H	H	H	H	H	H	H	H	H	H
9	H	H	H	H	H	H	H	H	H	H
10	D	D	D	D	D	D	D	D	H	H
11	D	D	D	D	D	D	D	D	D	H
12	H	H	S	S	S	H	H	H	H	H
13	S	S	S	S	S	H	H	H	H	H
14	S	S	S	S	S	H	H	H	H	H
15	S	S	S	S	S	H	H	H	H	H
16	S	S	S	S	S	H	H	H	H	H
A2	H	H	H	H	H	H	H	H	H	H
A3	H	H	H	H	H	H	H	H	H	H
A4	H	H	H	H	H	H	H	H	H	H
A5	H	H	H	H	H	H	H	H	H	H
A6	H	H	H	H	H	H	H	H	H	H
A7	S	S	S	S	S	S	S	H	H	H
A8	S	S	S	S	S	S	S	S	S	S
A9	S	S	S	S	S	S	S	S	S	S
22	H	H	Spl.	Spl.	Spl.	Spl.	H	H	H	H
33	H	H	Spl.	Spl.	Spl.	Spl.	H	H	H	H
66	H	Spl.	Spl.	Spl.	Spl.	H	H	H	H	H
77	Spl.	Spl.	Spl.	Spl.	Spl.	Spl.	H	H	H	H
88	Spl.	Spl.	Spl.	Spl.	Spl.	Spl.	Spl.	Spl.	Spl.	Spl.
99	Spl.	Spl.	Spl.	Spl.	Spl.	S	Spl.	Spl.	S	S
AA	Spl.	Spl.	Spl.	Spl.	Spl.	Spl.	Spl.	Spl.	Spl.	Spl.

H = Hit   S = Stand   D = Double   Spl. = Split

Chart 15
Master Chart
Las Vegas Multiple Deck

	2	3	4	5	6	7	8	9	10	A
8	H	H	H	H	H	H	H	H	H	H
9	H	D	D	D	D	H	H	H	H	H
10	D	D	D	D	D	D	D	D	H	H
11	D	D	D	D	D	D	D	D	D	H
12	H	H	S	S	S	H	H	H	H	H
13	S	S	S	S	S	H	H	H	H	H
14	S	S	S	S	S	H	H	H	H	H
15	S	S	S	S	S	H	H	H	H	H
16	S	S	S	S	S	H	H	H	H	H
A2	H	H	H	D	D	H	H	H	H	H
A3	H	H	H	D	D	H	H	H	H	H
A4	H	H	D	D	D	H	H	H	H	H
A5	H	H	D	D	D	H	H	H	H	H
A6	H	D	D	D	D	H	H	H	H	H
A7	S	D	D	D	D	S	S	H	H	H
A8	S	S	S	S	S	S	S	S	S	S
A9	S	S	S	S	S	S	S	S	S	S
22	H	H	Spl.	Spl.	Spl.	Spl.	H	H	H	H
33	H	H	Spl.	Spl.	Spl.	Spl.	H	H	H	H
66	H	Spl.	Spl.	Spl.	Spl.	H	H	H	H	H
77	Spl.	Spl.	Spl.	Spl.	Spl.	Spl.	H	H	H	H
88	Spl.	Spl.	Spl.	Spl.	Spl.	Spl.	Spl.	Spl.	Spl.	Spl.
99	Spl.	Spl.	Spl.	Spl.	Spl.	S	Spl.	Spl.	S	S
AA	Spl.	Spl.	Spl.	Spl.	Spl.	Spl.	Spl.	Spl.	Spl.	Spl.

H = Hit   S = Stand   D = Double   Spl. = Split

Atlantic City Multiple Deck

The blackjack games offered in Atlantic City differ from the Nevada games in several ways. For one thing, all the Atlantic City games are dealt from a six deck shoe. They do not offer single, double and four deck games as in Nevada. Doubling allowed after splitting is standard in Atlantic City as opposed to Nevada, where only a few casinos offer this option. Resplitting of pairs is not allowed in Atlantic City. Nevada casinos generally allow the player to resplit pairs as often as they wish.

The Atlantic City game is peculiar in some other ways as well. To protect against collusion between the player and the dealer, the dealer does not check his hole card for a blackjack (as is standard in Nevada) until all the players have finished playing out their hands. This casino safeguard does not affect the player's chances of winning, for if the dealer does indeed have a blackjack, any additional money the player may have wagered on a doubled or split hand will be returned. Only the original bet is lost.

Another difference is that all player hands are dealt face up in Atlantic City. No casinos allow the player to physically handle the cards. The player must employ hand signals to convey his strategy intentions to the dealer. (Single and double deck games in Nevada are generally face down games where the player can handle his cards, while multiple deck games are played similarly to the Atlantic City face up game.) Also, the minimum age to gamble is only 18 in Atlantic City as compared to 21 in Nevada.

The Atlantic City basic strategy is the same as Nevada multiple deck strategy except for more frequent pair splitting due to the player being allowed to double after splits.

Chart 16
Master Chart
Atlantic City (Multiple Deck)

	2	3	4	5	6	7	8	9	10	A
8	H	H	H	H	H	H	H	H	H	H
9	H	D	D	D	D	H	H	H	H	H
10	D	D	D	D	D	D	D	D	H	H
11	D	D	D	D	D	D	D	D	D	H
12	H	H	S	S	S	H	H	H	H	H
13	S	S	S	S	S	H	H	H	H	H
14	S	S	S	S	S	H	H	H	H	H
15	S	S	S	S	S	H	H	H	H	H
16	S	S	S	S	S	H	H	H	H	H
A2	H	H	H	D	D	H	H	H	H	H
A3	H	H	H	D	D	H	H	H	H	H
A4	H	H	D	D	D	H	H	H	H	H
A5	H	H	D	D	D	H	H	H	H	H
A6	H	D	D	D	D	H	H	H	H	H
A7	S	D	D	D	D	S	S	H	H	H
A8	S	S	S	S	S	S	S	S	S	S
A9	S	S	S	S	S	S	S	S	S	S
22	Spl.	Spl.	Spl.	Spl.	Spl.	Spl.	H	H	H	H
33	Spl.	Spl.	Spl.	Spl.	Spl.	Spl.	H	H	H	H
44	H	H	H	Spl.	Spl.	H	H	H	H	H
66	Spl.	Spl.	Spl.	Spl.	Spl.	H	H	H	H	H
77	Spl.	Spl.	Spl.	Spl.	Spl.	Spl.	H	H	H	H
88	Spl.	Spl.	Spl.	Spl.	Spl.	Spl.	Spl.	Spl.	Spl.	Spl.
99	Spl.	Spl.	Spl.	Spl.	Spl.	S	Spl.	Spl.	S	S
AA	Spl.	Spl.	Spl.	Spl.	Spl.	Spl.	Spl.	Spl.	Spl.	Spl.

H = Hit   S = Stand   D = Double   Spl. = Split

Chart 17
PLAYER'S OPTIONS

Player's Options Chart
These tables are to be used where the following variations are permitted:

Doubling Down Permitted After Splitting
A standard option in Atlantic City, but offered only in a few Nevada casinos. It allows the player to double down on one or more of the hands resulting from a split according to the standard doubling rules of the casino. This option allows us to split more aggressively so that we may take advantage of good doubling situations that can arise as a consequence of the split. This option is favorable to the player.

Our Hand		Single Deck	Multiple Deck
22	split against	2-7	2-7
33	split against	2-7	2-7
44	split against	4-6	5-6
66	split against	2-7	2-6
77	split against	2-8	2-7

Late Surrender (Surrender)
A player option to forfeit his hand and lose half his bet after it has been determined that the dealer does not have a blackjack. This option is favorable to the player.

Our Hand		Single Deck	Multiple Deck
16*	surrender against	10, A	9, 10, A
15	surrender against	10	10
77	surrender against	10	—

*Do not surrender 88 (split)

Early Surrender
A player option to forfeit his hand and lose half his bet before the dealer checks for a blackjack. An extremely valuable option for the player. No longer offered in Atlantic City.

Dealer's Upcard		Player's Totals
A	early surrender with	5-7, 12-17
10	early surrender with	14-16
9	early surrender with	16*

Do not surrender soft totals.
*Do not early surrender 88 (split).

V. THE WINNING EDGE

The removal of cards during play and the continued dealing from a deck depleted of these used cards creates a situation in blackjack where the odds of receiving particular cards or combinations of those cards constantly change during the course of the game. Computer studies have found that the removal of certain cards during play gives the player an advantage over the house, while the removal of others gives the house an advantage over the player.

Therefore, as cards are removed from play, the player's chances of winning constantly change. Sometimes the depleted deck of cards will favor the house and sometimes the player. By learning to analyze a depleted deck of cards for favorability, and capitalizing on this situation by betting more when the remaining cards are in your favor, you can actually have an edge over the casino.

The heart of all winning systems at blackjack is based on this theory—Bet more when you have the advantage, and less when the house has the advantage. This way, when you win, you win more, and when you lose, you lose less. Beginning with an even game (playing accurate basic strategy), this "maximize gain, minimize loss" betting strategy will give the player an overall edge on the house.

How do we determine when we have the edge? Computer studies have determined that 10s and Aces are the most valuable cards for the player, while the small cards, 2 through 7, are the most valuable cards for the house, 8s and 9s being relatively neutral. Off the top of the deck, with all cards still in play, the player has an even game with the house—neither side enjoys an advantage.*

The odds shift in favor of the player when there is a higher ratio of 9s, 10s and As in the deck than normal, and shift in favor of the house when there is a higher ratio of small cards, 2 through 7, than normal. All counting systems base their winning strategies on keeping track of the ratio of high cards to low cards. The systems vary in complexity from the very simple to the very complicated, all being based on the same principle—betting more when there is a higher proportion of

---

*Assuming the player plays perfect basic strategy, and that the game is a single deck game with the favorable Las Vegas Strip rules. If the particular game has less liberal rules (Northern Nevada) or is a multiple deck game, the house will enjoy a slight initial edge.

high cards in the deck.

However, there are many blackjack players that wish to have an edge over the house but are loathe to learn counting systems. For the player that desires to win without counting cards, the Cardoza School of Blackjack has developed some simple but effective techniques.

The Cardoza Non-Counter's Edge

The system is simple. All you need to know is that the high cards favor us and the small cards favor the house. When there are more high cards in the deck than normal, you will bet more. But you need not count cards. All you need to do is to keep your eyes open and watch the cards, just as you probably do anyway.

Here are 5 easy guidelines for the non-counter to have an edge:

1—When a great many small cards have been played in the first round, it is to the player's advantage. Bet 3 or 4 units instead of your normal 1 or 2 unit bet. (If $5 is your standard bet, then $15 is considered a 3 unit bet.)

Example—The following cards have been played. You had an 8, 5, 6, the player to your left had 10, 6, 2, another player had 10, 6, 5 and the dealer had a 10, 7. A disproportionate of small cards have been played, meaning the remaining cards are richer in high cards—to the player's advantage. So you bet more.

2—If on succeeding rounds, you estimate that there are still a disproportionate number of high cards remaining, continue to bet at a higher level than your minimum or neutral bet. Through practical experience, you will be able to improve on your estimation abilities.

3—If the cumulative distribution of cards seems to be fairly normal after a round of play, bet your neutral or minimum bet. (1 or 2 units, whatever your preference is.) If, however, you notice that no Aces have appeared, increase your bet by one unit. Your potential to get a blackjack has increased. While the dealer's chances of getting a blackjack has increased as well, he only gets paid even-money; you get paid 3 to 2.

4—On the other hand, if a disproportionate number of high cards appear in the first round, then place your minimum 1 unit bet, for the house has an edge. And if on succeeding rounds you judge that there is still a disproportionate number of small cards remaining, continue to place your minimum bets.

5—If the cumulative distribution of cards appears to be normal and you notice that more Aces have appeared than what you normally would expect (one Ace for every 13 cards is the normal composition), you want to downgrade your bet to one unit if you had been making 2 unit bets.

To sum up, when there are more 10s and Aces remaining in the deck than normal, increase your bet. When there are fewer 10s and Aces than normal (meaning more small cards than normal), decrease your bet. Every time the deck is shuffled, start your estimation of favorability over again.

Bet Range

I recommend a bet range of 1-4 units. Thus, if $5 is your standard bet, your maximum bet should not exceed $20. This is an important guideline to adhere to for several reasons:

1—Your advantage will rarely be large enough to warrant a bet larger than 4 units. We have bankroll limitations to consider, and do not want greed to be our downfall. Keep in mind that blackjack is a slow grind for the good players.

2) Raising your bets in advantageous situations to a range greater than 1-4 will attract undue attention to you as a skillful player, and the casino may begin to shuffle every time you make a large bet, in effect shuffling away advantageous situations.

3—You do not want to have one extremely large losing bet destroy an otherwise good session at the table.

4—The losing of a huge bet will generally have a very detrimental effect on your confidence, your concentration and your ability to think clearly. You will be surprised at how fast this can affect your physical and psychological frame of being.

5—The ranging of your bets from 1 unit in disadvantageous situations to 4 units in highly advantageous situations is a wide enough bet spread to maximize your gains while at the same time minimizing your risk.

The Power of Our Advantage

The Cardoza Non-Counter strategy gives the player an advantage powerful enough to give the $5-$20 bettor close to a $100 profit expectancy in a heavy weekend of play in a single deck game, and the $25-$100 bettor a $500 expectancy of winning. Now that you have the winning edge on the house, time will work to your advantage. The longer you play, the more money you can expect to make.

The advantage of the Cardoza Non-Counter strategy is that you can win with much less mental effort than the counting systems require, and can have fun at the same time! Obviously we cannot win as much without counting cards, but we will win.

Those readers desiring to further their edge over the house in blackjack, and to increase their profit expectancy, must learn a counting system. See back page for information on how to obtain the highly effective but simple to use Cardoza Base Count strategy.

Getting the Most out of the Cardoza Non-Counter Strategy

For those players that will be playing in Nevada, it will be to your advantage to play in a single deck game rather than multiple deck one for the following two reasons.

1—The single deck game is inherently more favorable.

2—The Cardoza Non-Counter strategy is most effective in a single deck game because the single deck game is highly sensitive to composition changes.

As to Atlantic City: The recent revocation of the early surrender rule there no longer gives the Basic Strategy player an edge over the house. The only way to beat the Atlantic City game at the present time is to learn a count strategy.

Tipping

Tipping, or toking, as it is called in casino parlance, should be viewed as a gratuitous gesture by the player to a dealer he feels has given him good service. Toking is totally at the player's discretion, and in no way should be considered an obligation. It is not the player's duty to support casino employees.

If you toke, toke only when you're winning, and only to dealers that are friendly and helpful to you. Do not toke dealers that you don't like or ones that try to make you feel guilty about not tipping. Dealers that make playing an unpleasant experience for you deserve nothing.

The best way to tip a dealer is to place a bet for the dealer in front of your own bet, so that his chances of winning that toke are tied up with your hand. If the hand is won, you both win together; if the hand is lost, you lose together. By being partners on the hand, you establish camaraderie with the dealer. Naturally, he will be rooting for you to win. This is the best way to tip, for when you win, the dealer wins double—the amount you bet for him, plus the winnings from that bet.

Cheating

It is my belief that cheating is not a problem in the major American gambling centers, though I would not totally eliminate the possibility. If you ever feel uncomfortable about the honesty of a game, stop playing. Though you probably are being dealt an honest game, the anxiety of being uncomfortable is not worth the action.

Do not confuse bad luck with being cheated, or a dealer's mistake as chicanery. Dealers have a difficult job and work hard. They are bound to make honest mistakes. If you find yourself shorted on a payoff, bring it immediately to the dealer's attention and the mistake will be corrected.

Understanding the Gamble

One of the realities of any gambling proposition is that no matter how well an individual plays a game, if chance is involved there will be times when the player will experience terrible runs of bad luck. There is no way to predict when these runs will begin, how long they will last or when they will stop.

It is important to understand that just because you have an advantage over the house, it does not mean you will win every time. Having a bad losing streak is not necessarily a reflection on your playing abilities. Even the best players take beatings on occasion. With a small advantage in blackjack, the skillful player will be vulnerable to dizzying streaks of luck, both good and bad.

However, if a skill factor is involved in the gambling proposition, as in blackjack, that factor will eventually make the skillful player a winner. The bettor that sticks by his guns when things go poorly will find tremendous rewards when things go his way, for, in the end, a player with the skills of winning will be way ahead of the game, a big winner.

VI. MONEY MANAGEMENT

Winning at blackjack requires not only the playing of the correct strategies but also the intelligent use of one's monetary resources. Blackjack is a very streaky game, and you can expect big winning and big losing streaks.

To emerge a winner from these pendulous swings of fortune takes a certain degree of emotional control, for the temptation to ride a winning streak too hard in the hopes of a big killing or to bet wildly during a losing streak, trying for a quick comeback, are two of the commonest factors that destroy a lot of gamblers. Inevitably the big winning sessions quickly dissipate into small wins or even disastrous losses while moderately bad losing sessions can turn into a nightmare.

Read this section carefully, for the difference between a player ending up a winner or a loser is heavily influenced by his skills in managing his money intelligently. Money management skills can be divided into the following categories:

a. Bankrolling (Total bankroll, table bankroll).

b. When to Quit (Maximize gains, minimize losses).

Before we look at these skills more closely, there is one extremely important point that must be thoroughly understood.

NEVER GAMBLE WITH MONEY YOU CANNOT AFFORD TO LOSE EITHER FINANCIALLY OR EMOTIONALLY. The importance of this rule cannot be overemphasized. Betting with money you cannot afford to lose will adversely affect your decision making. Rather than playing your game as optimally as you can, your strategy will be restricted according to the confines of your monetary or emotional situation. Betting with what is referred to as "scared money" is a good way to guarantee yourself a losing career as a gambler.

It is important to recognize that behind every bet is a human being. Recognizing that your emotions affect the quality of your play and acting accordingly is an important step toward making blackjack a pleasurable experience every time you play.

Sometimes you will not feel confident or alert for one reason or another. Accept that feeling. As a human being, you experience moods, and will not always feel at your best. But the important thing is to realize that you are physically or emotionally affected, and to act upon that realization and refrain from playing.

Whenever you feel emotionally unprepared to risk money, you should not play. When the playing of the game becomes a cause for anxiety, for whatever reason, and ceases to be a form of entertainment, then it is time to take a breather. You won't play as well because your mind will be preoccupied by the possibility of losing and perhaps more importantly, you will receive no emotional satisfaction from the game.

Play again later on, when you feel more alert and confident and you will have the necessary ingredients of a winner—emotional control. Remember the casinos aren't going anywhere.

Bankrolling

A. Total Bankroll

If you plan on being a successful blackjack player, your bankroll must be large enough to withstand the normal fluctuations common to blackjack. Under-capitalization and overbetting are the greatest dangers to the serious gambler. The player that consistently overbets will have larger winning sessions when he wins, but when he loses, he will lose big. And if that losing streak becomes extended, that player will be wiped out.

Playing with a bankroll large enough to sustain short run swings of bad luck is the only way to insure that your skill will bear long term results. The following bankroll requirements have been prepared to give the player enough capital to survive any reasonable losing streak, and be able to bounce back on top.

In the following table flat betting refers to betting the same amount every time. When ranging bets from 1-4, the player needs a larger bankroll, for more money is bet.

Chart 18
Bankroll Requirements

Hours to Play	Bet Range	Bankroll Needed
10	Flat	50 units
20+	Flat	100 units
10	1-4	150 units
20+	1-4	200 units

If you plan on playing for an extended weekend's worth of play (20 hours or more) at $5-$20 a hand, you should bring $1,000 with you, while if you are only planning to play 10 hours at those stakes, $750 will give you a fairly safe margin.

This does not mean that you will lose this money playing $5-$20. Using the Cardoza Non-Counter betting strategy, you will have an edge on the house, and your expectancy is to win money every time you go. However, it is important that the reader be aware that losing streaks occur, and the losing of $500-$600 is a possibility, though admittedly small. If the thought of losing amounts comparable to this during a downswing scares you, then you should not play $5-$20 a hand, for you are betting over your head.

Again, bet within your financial and emotional means, and you will never regret a single session at the tables.

If you have a definite amount of money to play with and want to figure out how much your unit size bet should be, simply take your gambling stake and divide it by the amount of units you need to have. Thus, if you bring $500 with you, and plan to play for 10 hours ranging your bets from 1-4, divide $500 by 150 units (see chart: bankroll needed column) and you will wager about $3 a hand. Betting more than $3 as a unit would be overbetting, and leaving yourself vulnerable to the risks discussed earlier.

B. Table Bankroll

How much money should you bring to the table?

My recommendation is that you bring 30 units to the table each time you play. If playing $5 units, bring $150; if $2 units, bring $60. You can bring less if you want (if flat betting, 15 units will suffice; if ranging from 1-4, 20 will do), but do not bring more money to the table. 30 units is enough to cover normal swings, and you never want to lose more than that at a table.

When to Quit

What often separates the winners from the losers is—the winners, when winning, leave the table a winner, and when losing, restrict their losses to affordable amounts. Smart gamblers never allow themselves to get destroyed at the table.

As a player, you have one big advantage that, if used properly, will insure you success as a gambler—You can quit playing whenever you want to. To come out ahead, you must minimize your losses when you lose and maximize your gains when you win. This way, your winning sessions will eclipse your losing sessions and you will come out an overall winner.

A. Minimizing Losses

Here are some simple guidelines that , if followed, will save you a lot of money.

1—Limit your table losses to 20 units (30 at the most). If betting $5 chips, never lose more than $100 in any one session; if $2 units, then $40. Do not dig in for more money, and you can never be a big loser. Take a break, try again later. You never want to get into a position where losing so much in one session totally demoralizes you.

2—Never increase your bet range beyond your bankroll capabilities. In other words, always bet within your means.

3—Never increase your bet size to catch up and break even. Raising it will not change the odds of the game, nor will it change your luck. What it will do is make your chances of taking a terrible beating frighteningly high. As before, do not get into a position where losing so much in one session destroys any reasonable chance of coming out even. You can't win all the time. Rest awhile; you'll get them later.

Maximizing Gains

Once winning, the most important thing in blackjack is to walk away a winner. There is no worse feeling than to leave the table a loser after having been up a lot of money. Once your wins at a table have exceeded 20 units, put aside 10 units of your winnings, and play the other 10 units. If a losing streak ensues and you lose those 10 units, you have protected yourself. You walk away 10 units the winner.

Set no limit on your winning sessions. If your hot streak continues, keep putting wins aside into your "don't touch" pile. When your luck changes and you have lost that 10 unit buffer, you can quit a big winner.

Should you increase your bet size when winning?

If you would like to try for a bigger win, the answer is yes, go for it —but in moderation. Do not get overzealous for that leaves your hard-earned win vulnerable to a few big losses. Increase your bets gradually when winning, keeping in mind that the more you bet, the more you risk losing.

One more thing to keep in mind. Just because you may have won six hands in a row doesn't mean that you'll win your seventh bet. You can just as easily lose that hand as win it. The theory on betting more at "hot" tables sounds good, but nobody has ever made a living following that strategy, for mathematically, and in practice, only the odds of the game determine one's chances of winning a particular play, not the won or lost results from the previous play.

Learn your basic strategies perfectly, apply the Cardoza Non-Counter betting strategy and listen to the advice offered in this section and you will have the knowledge and skills to be a consistent winner at the 21 tables.

VII. GLOSSARY

Barring a Player—The exclusion of a player from the blackjack tables, when casino personnel feel a player is too skillful.

Basic Strategy—The optimal playing strategy for a particular set of rules and number of decks used, assuming the player has knowlege of only his own two cards and the dealer's upcard.

Black Chips—$100 chips.

Blackjack or Natural—An original two card holding consisting of an Ace and ten-value card. Also the name of the game.

Break—see Bust.

Burn Card—A card, usually from the top of the deck that is removed from play. The top card is traditionally burned after a fresh shuffle and before the cards are dealt.

Bust or Break—To exceed the total of 21, an automatic loser.

Card Counting—A method of keeping track of the cards already played so that knowledge of the remaining cards can be used to adjust strategies. A player that counts cards is called a card counter.

Composition of the Deck—A term used to describe the particular makeup of the cards remaining in the deck.

Composition Change—As cards are removed from the deck, the normal proportion of certain cards to other groups of cards change. This is called a composition change.

Dealer—The casino employee who deals the cards, makes the proper payoffs to winning hands and collects lost bets.

Doubling, Doubling Down—A player option to double the original bet after seeing his original two cards. If the player chooses this option, one additional card will be dealt.

Doubling after Splitting—Option offered in Atlantic City and in only a few Nevada casinos whereby the player is allowed to double down after splitting a pair (according to normal doubling rules).

Draw—see Hit.

Early Surrender—Option offered in Atlantic City until recently. Player had the option to forfeit the hand and lose half his bet before the dealer checked for a blackjack.

Exposed Card—See Upcard.

Eye in the Sky—Refers to the mirrors above the gaming table where the games are constantly supervised to protect both the player and the house from being cheated.

Face Card—Jack, Queen or King. Also known as Paint.

First Base—Seat closest to dealer's left. The first baseman acts upon his hand first.

Flat Bet—To bet the same amount every hand.

Hard Total—A hand without an Ace or if containing an Ace, where the Ace counts as only 1 point (10, 6, A).

Head On or Head to Head—Playing alone with the dealer.

High Roller—A player that wagers big money.

Hit—The act of drawing (requesting) a card from the dealer.

Hole Card—The dealer's unexposed downcard.

House—A term to denote the Casino.

Insurance—A side bet that can be made when the dealer shows an Ace. The player wagers up to half his original bet and gets paid 2 to 1 on that bet if the dealer shows a blackjack. If the dealer does not have a blackjack, the insurance bet is lost. Play continues as usual.

Marker—An IOU signed by a player with established credit at a casino.

Multiple Deck Game—Blackjack played with two or more decks of cards, usually referring to a 4 or 6 deck game.

Natural—See Blackjack.

Nickels—$5 chips, usually red in color.

Northern Nevada—Usually referring to Lake Tahoe and Reno but can include other casino locations in Northern Nevada.

Pat Card—A dealer upcard of 7 through Ace, that tends to give the dealer pat hands.

Pat Hand—A hand totalling 17-21.

Pit Boss—Casino employee who supervises play at the gaming tables.

Push—A tie between the dealer and the player. Neither side wins.

Quarters—$25 chips, usually green in color.

Shoe—An oblong box used to hold multiple decks of cards. All 4 and 6 deck games are dealt out of a shoe.

Shuffle, Shuffling Up—The mixing of cards by a dealer prior to a fresh round of play.

Silver—$1 tokens or dollar chips.

Single Deck Game—Blackjack played from a single pack of cards.

Soft Hand, Soft Total—Hand in which the Ace counts as 11 points.

Splitting Pairs—A player option to split two cards of identical value so that two separate hands are formed. A bet equal to the original wager is placed next to the second hand.

Stiff Card—A dealer upcard of 2 through 6, that leaves the dealer with a high busting potential.

Stiff Hand—A hand totalling hard 12, 13, 14, 15 or 16; can be busted if hit.

Stand, Stand Pat—A player's decision not to draw a card.

Surrender, Late Surrender—A player option to forfeit his original hand and lose half the bet after it has been determined that the dealer does not have a blackjack. Option offered in only a few Nevada casinos.

Ten Factor—Refers to the high concentration of tens in the deck.

Ten-Value Card—10, Jack, Queen or King.

Third Base—Also called Anchorman. Position closest to dealer's right. The third baseman makes the last play before the dealer's turn.

Toke or Tip—A gratuity either given or bet for the dealer.

Unit—Bet size used as a standard of measurement.

Upcard—The dealer's face up (exposed) card.

Cardoza School of Blackjack

The Cardoza School of Blackjack is an institute that boasts well over a hundred students actively winning in casinos around the world. Graduates of the school have won into the 6 figures, and continue to win more every day.

The courses at the school are practical—students learn the techniques and strategies of winning casino blackjack, and will be able to consistently beat single and multiple deck games. Courses are available for beginning, intermediate and advanced players, and if the complete course is taken, the graduate will possess all the skills necessary to make him or her a professional blackjack player.

These skills include special psychological and emotional training to insure longevity as a successful player. Careful attention is given to preventing the casinos from ever discovering that the graduate is an expert. Many of the winning techniques taught at the Cardoza School of Blackjack are unavailable anywhere else.

For those players wishing private instruction, Mr. Cardoza can fly to their home city if prior arrangements are made. He is also available for lectures and seminars.

To find out more about the school, or Mr. Cardoza's services as a private instructor or lecturer, please write to:

The Cardoza School of Blackjack
P.O. Box 5267
Santa Cruz, California 95063

The complete course can also be taken by mail at a cost of $125 and includes the Cardoza Base Count Strategy. Students have found that the price of their tuition pays for itself over and over again in winnings. You will too!

ORDER NOW!

Please rush me the course by mail! Enclosed is a check or money order for $125. I want to join the hundreds of successful graduates making big money at blackjack!

NAME _____

ADDRESS _____

CITY _____ STATE _____ZIP _____